Published by Collins
An imprint of HarperCollins Publishers
HarperCollins Publishers
Westerhill Road
Bishopbriggs
Glasgow G64 2QT

www.harpercollins.co.uk

HarperCollins Publishers
Macken House,
39/40 Mayor Street Upper,
Dublin 1, D01 C9W8
Ireland

10 9 8 7 6 5 4 3 2 1

Some puzzles supplied by Clarity Media Ltd
All images © Shutterstock.com

ISBN 978-0-00-859952-2

Printed and bound in the UK using 100% renewable electricity at CPI Group (UK) Ltd

Publisher: Michelle l'Anson
Project Manager: Sarah Woods
Designer: Kevin Robbins

With more than 120 fun puzzles, you'll
never want to put this book down!

You can do them in any order, but all the two-player
games are in the first half of the book and all the
one-player games are in the second half of the book.

See if you have got the answers right by
checking them at the back of the book.

There are some blank pages too, which are
handy for jotting down workings, notes,
scribbles or whatever you like!

So... are you ready to

TWO-PLAYER GAMES

How to Play

This is a game for two players. The object of the game is to guess the correct word before all the parts of the dancing man have been drawn.

1. Each game has a subject, e.g. Animals. Player 1 thinks of a word that fits the subject. They draw a dash for each letter in the word.

_ _ _ _ _ _

| A | B | C | D | E | F | G | H | I | J | K | L | M |
| N | O | P | Q | R | S | T | U | V | W | X | Y | Z |

2. Player 2 says a letter that might be in the word and crosses off the letter on the alphabet at the bottom of the page. If the letter is in the word, Player 1 writes it above the correct dash.

_ A_ _ _ _

| A | B | C | D | E | F | G | H | I | J | K | L | M |
| N | O | P | Q | R | S | T | U | V | W | X | Y | Z |

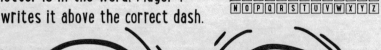

3. If the letter is not in the word. Player 1 draws one line on the dancing man.

_ **A** _ _ _

A̶	B	C	D	E	F	G	H	I	J	K	L	M
N	O̶	P	Q	R	S	T	U	V	W	X	Y	Z

4. Play continues with Player 2 guessing one letter at a time. Player 2 wins if they guess the correct word before all parts of the dancing man have been drawn. If they don't. Player 1 wins.

The subject is Nature...

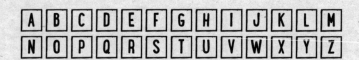

A B C D E F G H I J K L M
N O P Q R S T U V W X Y Z

DANCING MAN

The subject
is Transport...

A	B	C	D	E	F	G	H	I	J	K	L	M
N	O	P	Q	R	S	T	U	V	W	X	Y	Z

DANCING MAN

The subject is Food...

A B C D E F G H I J K L M
N O P Q R S T U V W X Y Z

DANCING MAN

The subject is Hobbies...

A B C D E F G H I J K L M
N O P Q R S T U V W X Y Z

DANCING MAN

The subject is Weather...

A B C D E F G H I J K L M
N O P Q R S T U V W X Y Z

DANCING MAN

The subject is Animals...

A B C D E F G H I J K L M
N O P Q R S T U V W X Y Z

How to Play

This is a game for two players. Each player will need to use a different coloured pen. The object of the game is to make the most boxes.

1. Player 1 connects one dot to another with a horizontal or vertical line.

2. Player 2 connects one dot to another with a horizontal or vertical line.

3. Players take turns connecting one dot to another. The aim is to complete a box. When a box is completed, that player writes their initial inside the box.

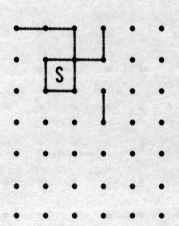

4. Play continues until all the dots are connected. The player with the most boxes at the end is the winner.

DOTS AND SQUARES

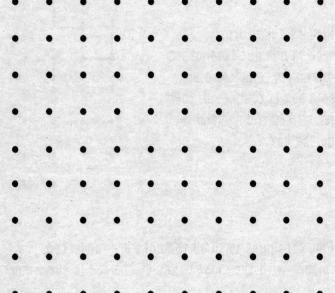

DOTS AND SQUARES

DOTS AND SQUARES

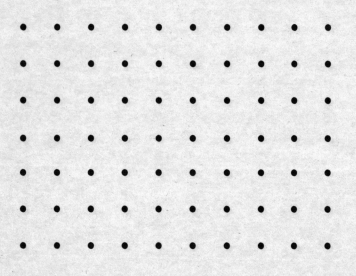

DOTS AND SQUARES

DOTS AND SQUARES

WORD GUESS

How to Play

This is a game for two players. The object of the game is to guess the word in six tries.

1. Player 1 thinks of a five-letter word.

2. Player 2 guesses a word and writes it into the first line of the grid.

3. Player 1 draws a circle around any letters that are in the answer word and in the correct place.

They draw a square around any letters that are in the answer word but in the wrong place.

For any letters that are not in the answer word, they put an X on the letter in the alphabet grid at the bottom of the page.

4. Player 2 guesses the word again and adds it to the next line of the grid.

5. Play continues. Player 2 has six tries to guess the word.

6. Player 2 scores points depending on how many tries they guessed the word in. For example, if they guessed the word in three tries they get 3 points. The aim is to get as low a score as possible!

G, R and T don't appear in the word.

G R E A T

E and A are in the word in the wrong place.

F and M don't appear in the word.

F L A M E

L, A and E are in the word in the correct place.

C does not appear in the word.

P L A C E

P, L, A and E are in the word in the correct place.

P L A N E

Well done! **PLANE** is the word. Score 4 points.

A B C D E F G H I J K L M
N O P Q R S T U V W X Y Z

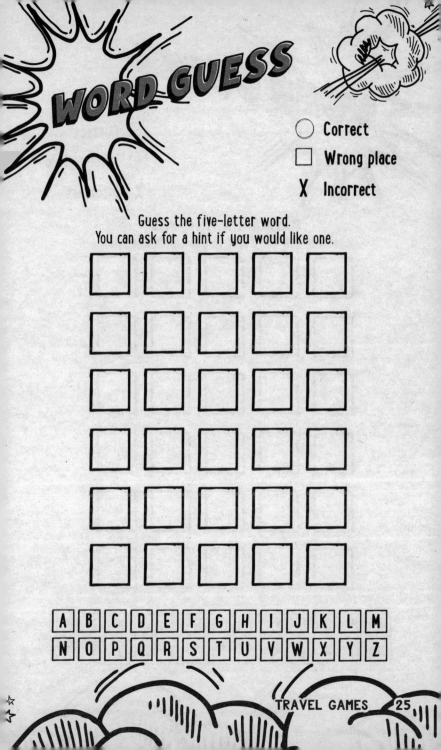

WORD GUESS

◯ Correct
☐ Wrong place
X Incorrect

Guess the five-letter word.
You can ask for a hint if you would like one.

| A | B | C | D | E | F | G | H | I | J | K | L | M |
| N | O | P | Q | R | S | T | U | V | W | X | Y | Z |

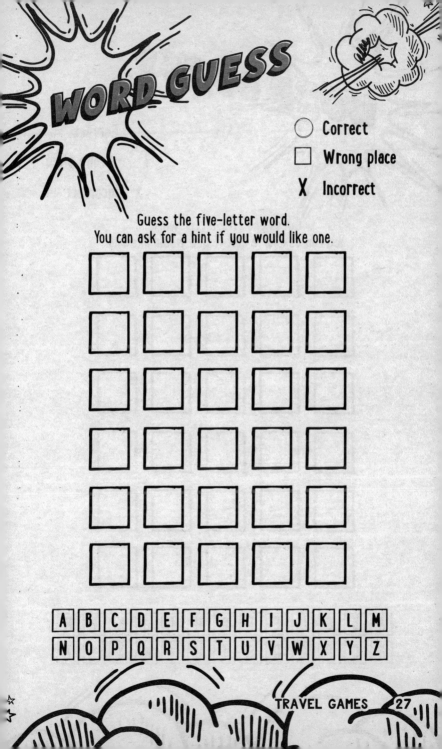

WORD GUESS

○ Correct

☐ Wrong place

X Incorrect

Guess the five-letter word.
You can ask for a hint if you would like one.

| A | B | C | D | E | F | G | H | I | J | K | L | M |
| N | O | P | Q | R | S | T | U | V | W | X | Y | Z |

28

How to Play

This is a game for two players. Each player will need a different coloured pen. The object of the game is to have the highest total score at the end of the game.

1. Player 1 draws a number 1 in any of the circles on the grid.

2. Player 2 draws a number 1 in any of the other circles on the grid.

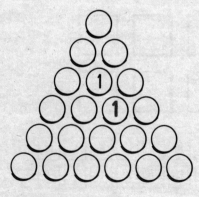

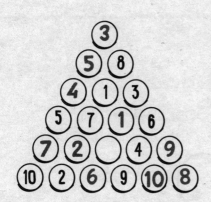

3. Players take turns adding their numbers into the circles. from 1 to 10. Numbers can be added in any order. but only once by each player.

PLAYER 1 - 46
PLAYER 2 - 35

4. After both players write 10. there is one circle left: the vortex. The vortex destroys all its neighbouring circles. The winner is the player whose remaining numbers add up to the highest score.

How to Play

This is a game for two players. The object of the game is to make a line of three of your symbols in a row.

1. Player 1 draws an X in any of the spaces of the grid.

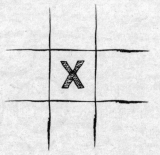

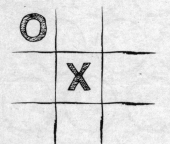

2. Player 2 draws an O in any of the other spaces of the grid.

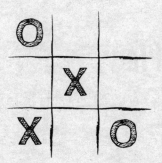

3. Players take turns drawing their symbols in the grid. The aim is to make a line of three symbols in a row – horizontally, vertically or diagonally.

4. The player who makes a line of three is the winner. They draw a line through the three symbols. If no one makes a line, the game is a tie.

NOUGHTS AND CROSSES

NOUGHTS AND CROSSES

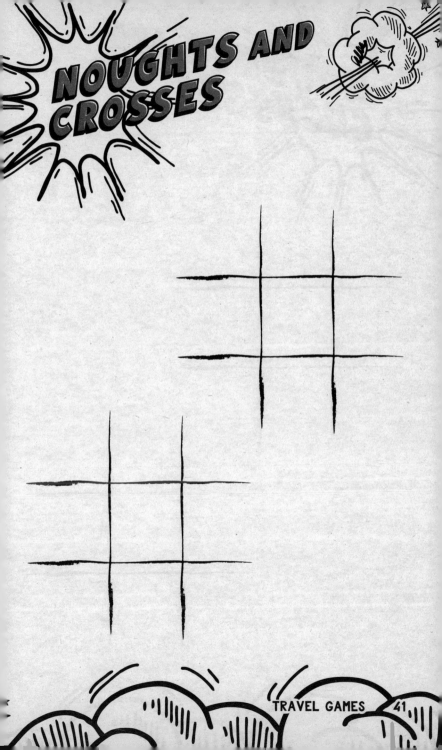

NOUGHTS AND CROSSES

NOUGHTS AND CROSSES

NOUGHTS AND CROSSES

NOUGHTS AND CROSSES

How to Play

This is a game for two players. Each player will need to use a different coloured pen. The object of the game is to NOT complete a triangle.

1. Player 1 draws one straight line on the hexagon from dot to dot.

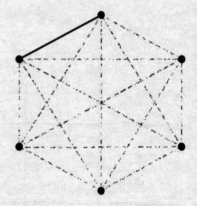

2. Player 2 draws a different line on the hexagon from dot to dot.

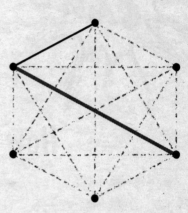

3. Players take turns drawing lines on the hexagon. The first player who completes a triangle made entirely of their own colour, loses the game. Only triangles with dots at each corner count.

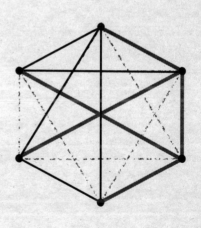

HEXAGON GAME

HEXAGON GAME

HEXAGON GAME

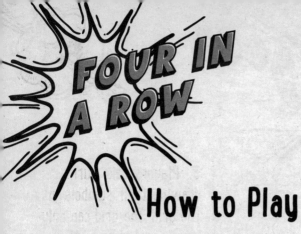

How to Play

This is a game for two players. The object of the game is to make a line of four of your symbols in a row.

1. Player 1 draws an X in any of the spaces on the bottom row of the grid.

2. Player 2 draws an 0 in any of the other spaces on the bottom row of the grid or above the X.

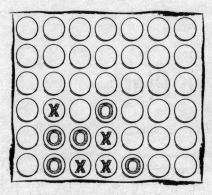

3. Players take turns drawing their symbols in the grid. The grid can only be completed from the bottom upwards.

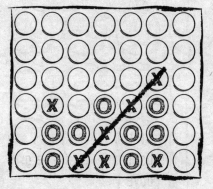

4. The winner is the first player to make a line of four of their symbols in a row – horizontally, vertically or diagonally.

FOUR IN A ROW

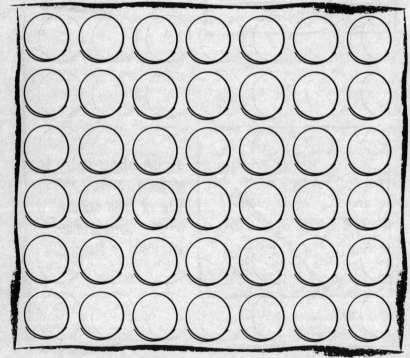

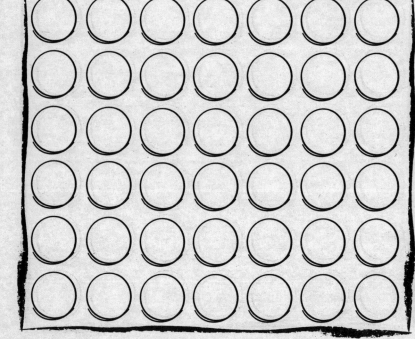

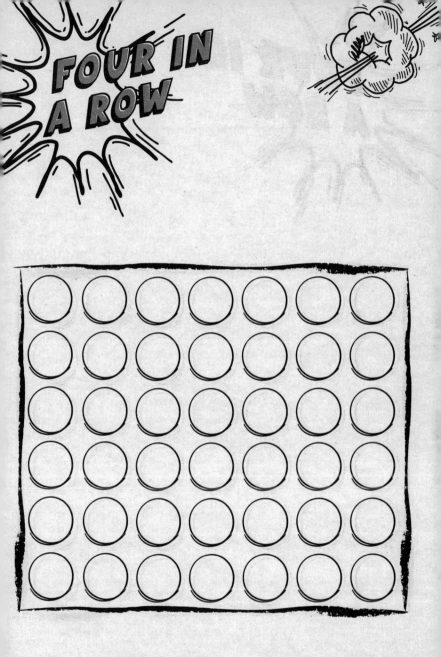

FOUR IN A ROW

FOUR IN A ROW

FOUR IN A ROW

How to Play

This is a game for two players. Each player will need to use a different coloured pen. The object of the game is to connect the most dots (draw the most lassos).

1. Player 1 draws a line from one dot to another dot and circles the dot at the end.

2. Player 2 draws a line from one dot to another dot and circles the dot at the end.

3. Players continue taking turns. They may start on a dot that has already been used as a starting point but they can only circle a dot that has not yet been used. Lines must stay within the grid and must not cross any other lines.

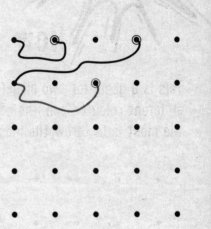

4. When there are no more available moves left, the game ends. The winner is the last person to draw a lasso.

LASSO

LASSO

LASSO

· · · · ·

· · · · ·

· · · · ·

· · · · ·

· · · · ·

· · · · ·

How to Play

1. This is a two-player game.

2. Each player takes a turn to add in a word starting with each letter of the alphabet for the subject of the puzzle.

3. The subject for the puzzle opposite is Insects.

4. We have started the puzzle off for you. Can you complete the rest of the alphabet?

The subject is Insects...

A	Ant	**N**	
B	Butterfly	**O**	
C	Caterpillar	**P**	
D		**Q**	
E		**R**	
F		**S**	
G		**T**	
H		**U**	
I		**V**	
J		**W**	
K		**X**	
L		**Y**	
M		**Z**	

ALPHABET GAME

The subject is Food...

A _____ N _____

B _____ O _____

C _____ P _____

D _____ Q _____

E _____ R _____

F _____ S _____

G _____ T _____

H _____ U _____

I _____ V _____

J _____ W _____

K _____ X _____

L _____ Y _____

M _____ Z _____

ALPHABET GAME

The subject
is Birds...

A _____   N _____
B _____   O _____
C _____   P _____
D _____   Q _____
E _____   R _____
F _____   S _____
G _____   T _____
H _____   U _____
I _____   V _____
J _____   W _____
K _____   X _____
L _____   Y _____
M _____   Z _____

ALPHABET GAME

The subject is Transport...

A _____
B _____
C _____
D _____
E _____
F _____
G _____
H _____
I _____
J _____
K _____
L _____
M _____

N _____
O _____
P _____
Q _____
R _____
S _____
T _____
U _____
V _____
W _____
X _____
Y _____
Z _____

ALPHABET GAME

The subject is Animals...

A _____   N _____
B _____   O _____
C _____   P _____
D _____   Q _____
E _____   R _____
F _____   S _____
G _____   T _____
H _____   U _____
I _____   V _____
J _____   W _____
K _____   X _____
L _____   Y _____
M _____   Z _____

ALPHABET GAME

The subject is Cities...

A _____   N _____
B _____   O _____
C _____   P _____
D _____   Q _____
E _____   R _____
F _____   S _____
G _____   T _____
H _____   U _____
I _____   V _____
J _____   W _____
K _____   X _____
L _____   Y _____
M _____   Z _____

ALPHABET GAME

The subject is Nature...

A _____   N _____
B _____   O _____
C _____   P _____
D _____   Q _____
E _____   R _____
F _____   S _____
G _____   T _____
H _____   U _____
I _____   V _____
J _____   W _____
K _____   X _____
L _____   Y _____
M _____   Z _____

ONE-PLAYER GAMES

QUIZ

Test your knowledge. Do you know which of the three choices is the right answer?

1. What does a helicopter usually take off from and land on?

a) Helipad b) Lily pad c) Notepad

2. What mode of transport is an airbus?

a) Bus b) Aeroplane c) Bicycle

3. In which area of an aeroplane would you typically find the pilot?

a) Cockpit b) Cabin c) Galley

4. Which of these might you hear as you get on a train?

a) 'Taxi!' b) 'All aboard!' c) 'Bingo!'

5. What is a helicopter sometimes called?

a) Cutter b) Slicer c) Chopper

6. Gliders are aircraft that do not have:

a) Wings b) Pilots c) Engines

7. Which of these is a famous transport system in Paris?

a) Motto b) Metro c) Pogo

8. Which of these does not have an engine?

a) Kayak b) Motorboat c) Speedboat

Place the numbers from 1-4 once in each row, column and 2x2 bold-outlined box.

MAZE

Can you find a route for each of the monsters to get to their friend in the middle of the maze and help them?

HELP!

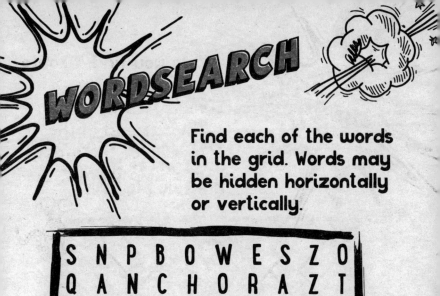

WORDSEARCH

Find each of the words in the grid. Words may be hidden horizontally or vertically.

S	N	P	B	O	W	E	S	Z	O
Q	A	N	C	H	O	R	A	Z	T
S	U	K	Q	A	Y	C	I	P	D
A	A	D	M	I	R	A	L	I	E
B	O	A	R	S	O	B	H	E	C
O	C	U	U	V	O	I	O	R	K
A	O	Z	T	I	A	N	J	B	M
R	E	C	A	P	T	A	I	N	A
D	I	J	E	T	T	Y	I	F	S
S	W	T	O	V	I	T	S	D	T

ABOARD	CABIN	MAST
ADMIRAL	CAPTAIN	OARS
ANCHOR	DECK	PIER
BOW	JETTY	SAIL

SPOT THE DIFFERENCE

Can you spot the seven differences between the two pictures?

WORDWHEEL

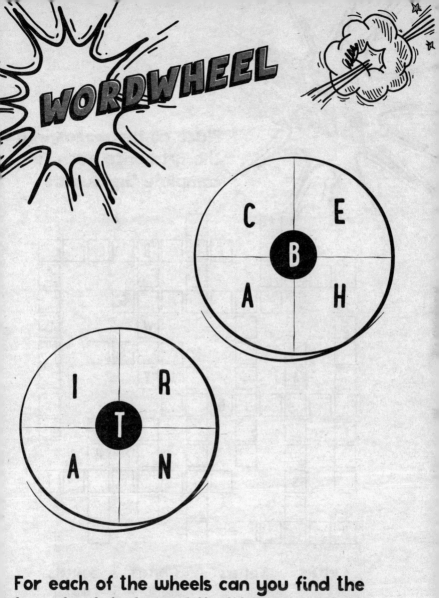

For each of the wheels can you find the travel-related word that begins with the centre letter and uses every letter in the wheel once?

KRISS KROSS

Place all the words into the grid once each to complete the puzzle.

4 letters
DESK
FOOD
FUEL
GATE
TAXI

5 letters
PILOT
SHOPS

6 letters
RUNWAY

7 letters
AIRLINE
BAGGAGE
LANDING
SEATING

8 letters
CAROUSEL
PASSPORT
SECURITY
TERMINAL
TOURISTS

ARROW WORD

Work out the answers to the clues and write them in the grid, following the arrows.

Sound a sheep makes	Large primate ▼	▼	Put on chips. ____ & vinegar	▼	Additional
▶	▼	A	A country in Europe		Finish
What you eat food off ▶	P	L	T ▼	T	E ▼
R ▶					N
Go back	Flower	Unhappy ▶		A	
▶	Y ▼			Unusual	Where you sleep
Pick up		Steal ▶	R ▶	O ▼	▼
D ▶	I				
Split into smaller parts		Sum numbers together ▶			D

TRAVEL GAMES 87

MISSING VOWELS

TCKT

DRVR

STTN

CNDCTR

PLTFRM

CRRGE

These six words have had their vowels removed. Can you add them back in to find the train-related words?

Test your knowledge. Do you know which of the three choices is the right answer?

1. What is New York City also known as?

a) The Curvy Pear   b) The Juicy Orange   c) The Big Apple

2. Where would you find the Eiffel Tower?

a) London   b) Paris   c) Barcelona

3. Which animal is the fastest?

a) Cheetah   b) Gazelle   c) Hyena

4. What colour are a zebra's stripes?

a) Black and white   b) Green and gold   c) Blue and white

5. How much of the planet is ocean?

a) Less than 30 %   b) Less than 50 %   c) More than 70 %

6. Fill in the blank: the _____ Tower of Pisa

a) Bending   b) Leaning   c) Curving

7. Which of these is a famous London landmark?

a) Big Ken   b) Big Ben   c) Big Len

8. In which country would you find the Great Pyramid of Giza?

a) Namibia   b) Thailand   c) Egypt

PAIRS MATCH

Can you find the two matching ships?
Circle the image and link it to its matching
pair with a line.

DOMINO MATCH

There is a game of dominoes laid out, but some of the dominoes are blank. Can you fill in the spots?

WORDSEARCH

Find each of the words in the grid. Words may be hidden horizontally or vertically.

A	D	V	E	N	T	U	R	E	W
C	O	O	K	I	N	G	W	U	A
T	C	T	R	A	I	L	I	H	L
S	A	T	E	N	T	O	J	I	K
I	M	L	L	R	Q	U	F	K	I
F	P	M	O	U	N	T	A	I	N
R	I	F	X	S	A	D	C	N	G
U	N	I	S	W	H	O	W	G	F
R	G	R	M	A	P	O	D	B	C
S	H	E	L	T	E	R	U	S	C

ADVENTURE	HIKING	SHELTER
CAMPING	MAP	TENT
COOKING	MOUNTAIN	TRAIL
FIRE	OUTDOOR	WALKING

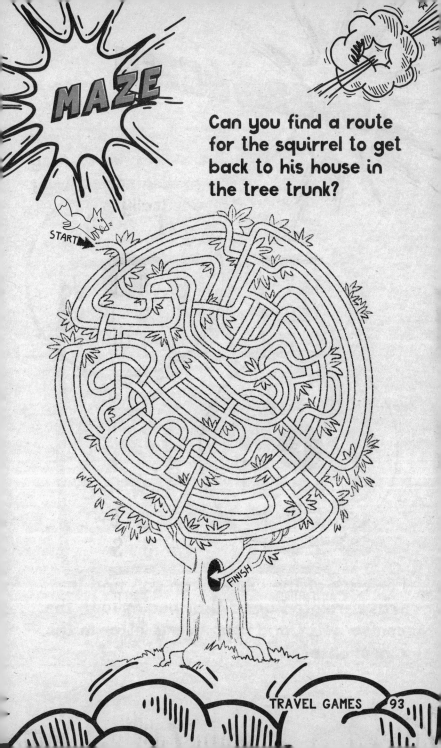

MAZE

Can you find a route for the squirrel to get back to his house in the tree trunk?

START

FINISH

WORDWHEEL

For each of the wheels can you find the travel-related word that begins with the centre letter and uses every letter in the wheel once?

KRISS KROSS

Place all the words into the grid once each to complete the puzzle.

4 letters	5 letters	7 letters	8 letters	9 letters
CHAD	EGYPT	ALGERIA	BOTSWANA	SINGAPORE
IRAN	GHANA	ARMENIA	MALAYSIA	
IRAQ	INDIA	LEBANON	PAKISTAN	**10 letters**
LAOS	SUDAN	TUNISIA		BANGLADESH

Test your knowledge. Do you know which of the three choices is the right answer?

1. Where is the famous Hollywood sign found?

a) California   b) Jamaica   c) Mexico

2. Which of these is a French pastry?

a) Bagel   b) Croissant   c) Strudel

3. What does the Statue of Liberty hold in her right hand?

a) A torch   b) A trophy   c) A flower

4. What is the name of a famous ship that sank in 1912?

a) RMS Queen Mary   b) RMS Titanic   c) HMS Colossus

5. What can helicopters do that jumbo jets can't?

a) Hover   b) Take off   c) Land

6. Name the unmanned aircraft that is controlled from the ground.

a) Moan   b) Drone   c) Clone

7. What do you sit on when travelling by horse?

a) A bench   b) A stool   c) A saddle

8. Which of these is able to submerge and operate underwater?

a) Ferry   b) Yacht   c) Submarine

SUDOKU 4X4

Place the numbers from 1-4 once in each row, column and 2x2 bold-outlined box.

DOMINO MATCH

There is a game of dominoes laid out, but some of the dominoes are blank. Can you fill in the spots?

MISSING VOWELS

PLT

FLGHT

CSTMS

LGGG

PSSPRT

SCRTY

These six words have had their vowels removed. Can you add them back in to find the airport-related words?

PAIRS MATCH

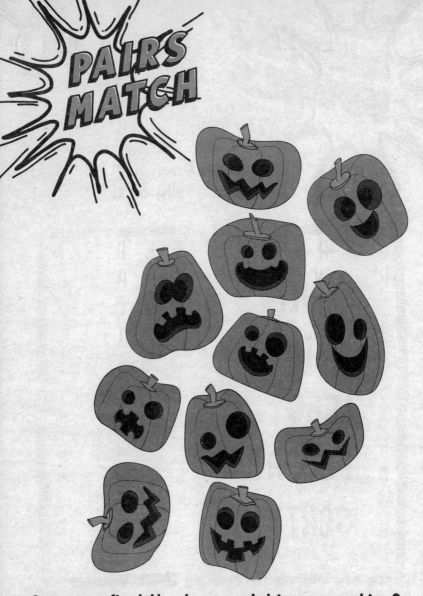

Can you find the two matching pumpkins? Circle the image and link it to its matching pair with a line.

WORDSEARCH

Find each of the words in the grid. Words may be hidden horizontally, vertically or diagonally.

G	O	R	L	O	B	S	T	E	R	U	K
P	C	W	A	R	F	S	S	L	R	A	R
W	T	O	A	H	L	H	W	Y	O	X	S
S	I	U	A	V	R	I	I	Z	C	J	L
C	X	N	R	S	E	N	M	S	K	S	I
S	R	L	D	T	T	G	M	Q	Z	S	F
A	O	A	P	Y	L	L	I	U	V	U	E
N	O	O	B	Q	R	E	N	I	H	S	G
D	G	S	L	D	U	N	G	D	O	U	U
J	E	L	L	Y	F	I	S	H	U	R	A
H	U	D	E	T	U	C	R	S	F	F	R
P	X	L	R	K	E	L	P	G	Q	A	D

COAST	KELP	ROCK	SQUID	TURTLE
CRAB	LIFEGUARD	SAND	SURF	WAVE
JELLYFISH	LOBSTER	SHINGLE	SWIMMING	WIND

ARROW WORD

Work out the answers to the clues and write them in the grid, following the arrows.

Birds that 'honk' ▼		Part of a plant ▼	Primary colour ▼	Sugary	A ▼
Arm joint ►		L	B	O	
Slippery fish ►			L	Job done for a long time ▼	
Red liquid 'tomato' _____ ►			U		
►D	E			A	
Lose	Large body of water	Cooking pot	What a hen lays	R	Not wet
Rate of movement ►	▼	▼	▼	E	▼
Keen ►		A			R
Annoyed ►		N			

102

QUIZ

Test your knowledge. Do you know which of the three choices is the right answer?

1. Which of these is a desert in Africa?

a) Sarah   b) Sahara   c) Savannah

2. Where would you find Machu Picchu?

a) Peru   b) Colombia   c) Paraguay

3. The flag of which country contains a maple leaf?

a) Mexico   b) Canada   c) Cuba

4. Which of these is in Asia?

a) Great Wall of China   b) Hollywood sign   c) Notre Dame

5. Which of these cities is found in Japan?

a) Athens   b) Tokyo   c) Lisbon

6. Which of these is the longest river in Africa?

a) River Nile   b) River File   c) River Mile

7. The leaves of which tree make up most of the diet of a koala?

a) Maple   b) Oak   c) Eucalyptus

8. Which river flows through South America?

a) Nile   b) Thames   c) Amazon

SPOT THE DIFFERENCE

Can you spot the ten differences between the two pictures?

104

DOMINO MATCH

There is a game of dominoes laid out, but some of the dominoes are blank. Can you fill in the spots?

KRISS KROSS

Place all the words into the grid once each to complete the puzzle.

3 letters
CAB

4 letters
HALT
LINE
STOP

5 letters
BRAKE
DEPOT
STAFF
TRACK

6 letters
DRIVER
PORTER
SIGNAL
TICKET

7 letters
ARRIVAL
EXPRESS
STATION

8 letters
PLATFORM
SCHEDULE

9 letters
CONDUCTOR

SUDOKU 4X4

Place the numbers from 1-4 once in each row, column and 2x2 bold-outlined box.

MAZE

Can you find a route for each of the pencils to get to the fish in the middle of the maze? You can colour them in when you have reached them.

WORDWHEEL

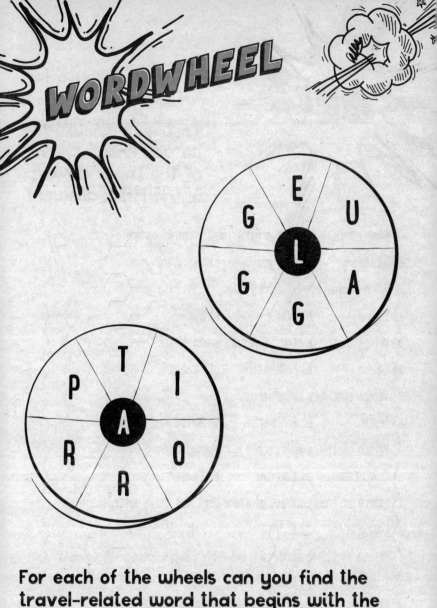

For each of the wheels can you find the travel-related word that begins with the centre letter and uses every letter in the wheel once?

**Test your knowledge.
Do you know which
of the three choices
is the right answer?**

1. What name is given to a luxurious form of camping?

a) Glumping   b) Glamping   c) Skimping

2. What colour are London's famous taxis?

a) Yellow   b) White   c) Black

3. Which of these might you use when on ice?

a) Canoe   b) Pogo stick   c) Skates

4. Which road has three lanes?

a) Track   b) Footpath   c) Motorway

5. Which of these is a pace a horse might move at?

a) Canter   b) Counter   c) Chaser

6. Which of these modes of transport has three wheels?

a) Unicycle   b) Bicycle   c) Tricycle

7. Which of these animals transports people across the desert?

a) Camel   b) Rhino   c) Deer

8. Where are you most likely to ride an elephant?

a) North America   b) South America   c) Asia

PAIRS MATCH

Can you match up the pairs of socks? Circle each image and link it to its matching pair with a line. There is an odd sock, which one is it?

WORDSEARCH

Find each of the words in the grid. Words may be hidden horizontally, vertically or diagonally.

```
G V U Q V I E W I N G F
F C H E E T A H P Y I I
T T F R G I R A F F E U
R V V U L Z A F R I C A
E R E W O E R S O I R O
B L R H I N O C E R O S
U Z E M I L S P K A L T
F E H P A C D R A Y E R
F B Y A H B L L L R N I
A R E R I A J E I L D C
L A N J A A N X O F N H
O B A B O O N T N K E L
```

AFRICA	CHEETAH	HYENA	OSTRICH	VIEWING
BABOON	ELEPHANT	LEOPARD	RHINOCEROS	WILDLIFE
BUFFALO	GIRAFFE	LION	VEHICLE	ZEBRA

MISSING VOWELS

HTL

RLX

TRVL

FMLY

SNSHN

SGHTS

These six words have had their vowels
removed. Can you add them back in to
find the holiday-related words?

WORDWHEEL

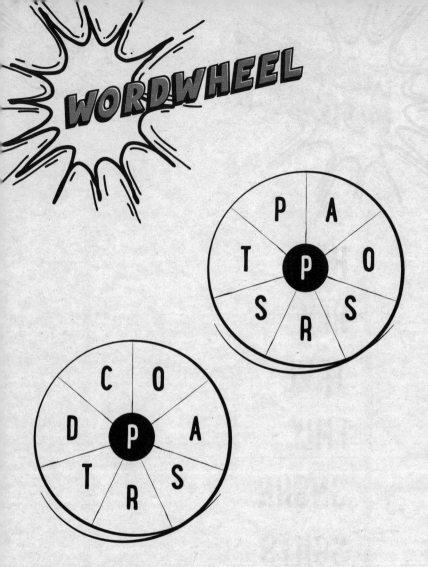

For each of the wheels can you find the travel-related word that begins with the centre letter and uses every letter in the wheel once?

ARROW WORD

Work out the answers to the clues and write them in the grid, following the arrows.

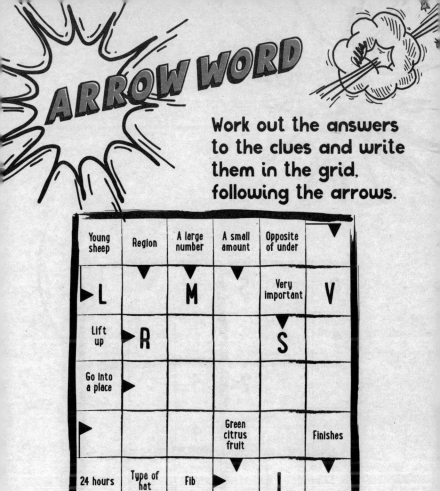

Young sheep	Region	A large number	A small amount	Opposite of under	▼
► L	▼	▼ M	▼	Very important	V
Lift up	R			▼ S	
Go into a place	►				
►			Green citrus fruit		Finishes
24 hours	Type of hat	Fib	► ▼	I	▼
►	▼				
Deed, or thing done		Dirt	►		D
Push	►		E		

SUDOKU
6X6

2		5			
4					3
		2	3		
		1	4		
1					4
			1		5

**Place the numbers from 1-6 once in each
row, column and 3x2 bold-outlined box.**

QUIZ

Test your knowledge. Do you know which of the three choices is the right answer?

1. What colour are London's famous buses?

a) Blue   b) Yellow   c) Red

2. Which of these is a national emblem of Wales?

a) Carrot   b) Leek   c) Parsnip

3. Where are the Crown Jewels kept?

a) Windsor Castle   b) The Tower of London   c) The London Eye

4. Where is Italy's famous leaning tower?

a) Palermo   b) Pisa   c) Pompeii

5. Where is Flamenco dancing popular?

a) Serbia   b) Spain   c) Slovakia

6. Which of these is the capital city of India?

a) Chennai   b) Pune   c) New Delhi

7. What is sourdough a type of?

a) Sweet   b) Bread   c) Chicken

8. The smallest country in South America is:

a) Brazil   b) Ecuador   c) Suriname

DOMINO MATCH

There is a game of dominoes laid out, but some of the dominoes are blank. Can you fill in the spots?

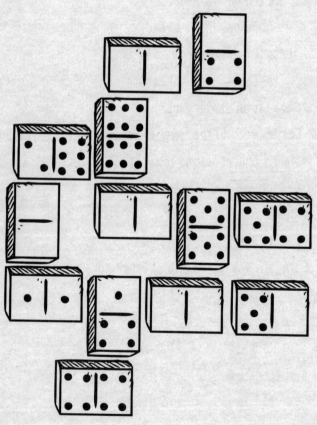

KRISS KROSS

Place all the words into the grid once each to complete the puzzle.

3 letters	5 letters	6 letters	7 letters	8 letters
FAN	ALARM	BUMPER	ANTENNA	HEADREST
	BRAKE	ENGINE	BATTERY	
4 letters	MOTOR	HEATER	EXHAUST	**9 letters**
AXLE	PEDAL	WASHER	GEARBOX	HEADLIGHT
DOOR			SUNROOF	

ARROW WORD

Work out the answers to the clues and write them in the grid, following the arrows.

Used to take photos	Precise	A planet	Long period of time	Argue	Every
▶	A				
Christmas song ▶		A	R		
Move on hands and knees ▶	C				
▶			Rip	A single time	Porridge grains
Form of public transport		Also ▶			
Sports venue ▶					
100 _____ sprint race		Take part in a play ▶		C	
▶					S

MISSING VOWELS

TRCK

SRVCS

RDWRKS

MTRWY

STBLT

CNTRYSD

These six words have had their vowels removed. Can you add them back in to find the roadtrip-related words?

MAZE

Can you work out which one of the monster's tentacles is catching the ball?

PAIRS MATCH

Can you find the two matching cacti? Circle the image and link it to its matching pair with a line.

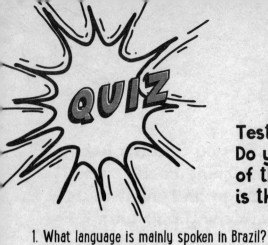

Test your knowledge. Do you know which of the three choices is the right answer?

1. What language is mainly spoken in Brazil?

a) Portuguese   b) Spanish   c) French

2. Which animal is known for jumping?

a) Kangaroo   b) Koala   c) Platypus

3. Which of these desserts is from America?

a) Bakewell tart   b) Key lime pie   c) Baklava

4. What colours are on the Japanese flag?

a) Black and blue   b) Red and white   c) Yellow and red

5. What is Uluru?

a) A sandstone rock   b) A dance   c) A food

6. Which of these is an enclosed area for skating?

a) Rank   b) Drink   c) Rink

7. Which of these landmarks is the tallest?

a) Leaning Tower of Pisa   b) Big Ben   c) Eiffel Tower

8. When a submarine needs to see above water, what does it use?

a) Periscope   b) Telescope   c) Goggles

WORDWHEEL

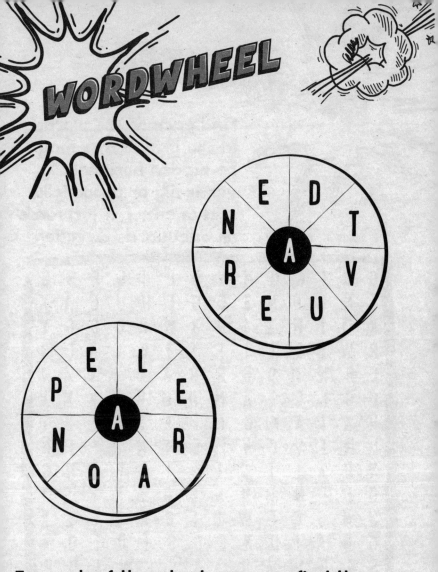

For each of the wheels can you find the travel-related word that begins with the centre letter and uses every letter in the wheel once?

WORDSEARCH

Find each of the words in the grid. Words may be hidden horizontally, vertically or diagonally and in either a forwards or backwards direction.

```
G S I G U N Y U L J G E S S
E N G P N S C G L H J C A K
X O I N S I R J W R U G G Y
P W G W I T F T I B C N C D
L B N N O B R R A U I I A I
O O I C I R M D U R X K M V
R A T A K D I I E S G A P I
I R F V C V I E L N J Y I N
N D A I I S T L I C E A N G
G I R N T N F E G T K K G I
N N G G E W O E J A Q C Z X
G G A I Q N E Q S T R T O X
S L R W A R Q A S I W A Q R
R O Z C C Y C L I N G X P S
```

CAMPING	CYCLING	ORIENTEERING	ROCK CLIMBING	SKYDIVING
CANOEING	EXPLORING	PARAGLIDING	ROWING	SNOWBOARDING
CAVING	KAYAKING	RAFTING	SCUBA DIVING	SURFING

SUDOKU 6X6

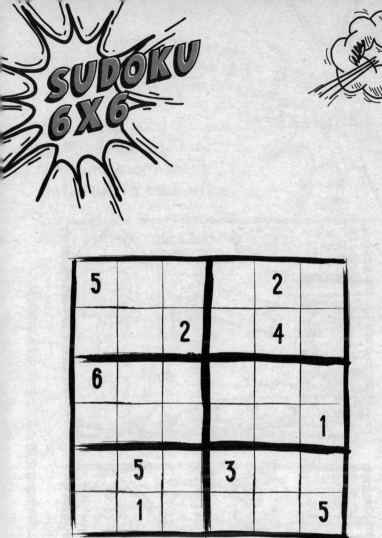

Place the numbers from 1-6 once in each row, column and 3x2 bold-outlined box.

SPOT THE DIFFERENCE

Can you spot the ten differences between the two pictures?

128

ARROW WORD

Work out the answers to the clues and write them in the grid, following the arrows.

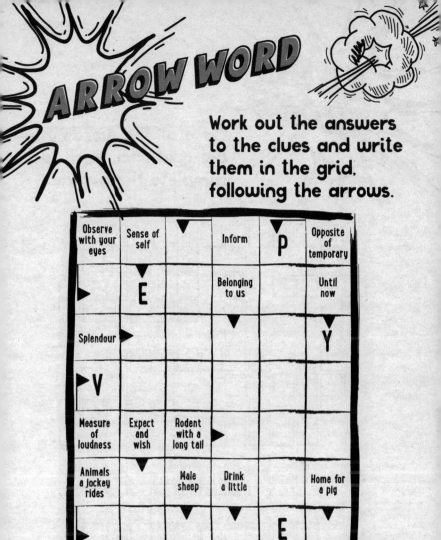

Observe with your eyes	Sense of self	▼	Inform	▼ P	Opposite of temporary
	▼ E		Belonging to us		Until now
Splendour ▶			▼		▼ Y
▶ V					
Measure of loudness	Expect and wish	Rodent with a long tail	▶		
Animals a jockey rides	▼	Male sheep	Drink a little		Home for a pig
▶		▼	▼	E	▼
Used by artists ▶					
Vacant ▶				T	

KRISS KROSS

Place all the words into the grid once each to complete the puzzle.

3 letters
BED
GYM
SPA

4 letters
MENU
POOL
ROOM
SAFE
STAY

5 letters
CHAIR
SAUNA

6 letters
GUESTS
LUXURY
RESORT

7 letters
BELLHOP
HOLIDAY
MANAGER

8 letters
BATHROOM

9 letters
BREAKFAST

10 letters
RESTAURANT

MISSING VOWELS

WVS

TWL

SHLL

PRSL

SN CRM

SNDCSTL

These six words have had their vowels removed. Can you add them back in to find the beach-related words?

DOMINO MATCH

There is a game of dominoes laid out, but some of the dominoes are blank. Can you fill in the spots?

PAIRS MATCH

Can you find the two matching parrots? Circle the image and link it to its matching pair with a line.

Page 80 – Quiz

1. a – Helipad
2. b – Aeroplane
3. a – Cockpit
4. b – 'All Aboard!'
5. c – Chopper
6. c – Engines
7. b – Metro
8. a – Kayak

Page 81 – Sudoku

4	2	3	1
3	1	4	2
2	4	1	3
1	3	2	4

4	3	1	2
1	2	4	3
3	4	2	1
2	1	3	4

Page 82 – Maze

Page 83 – Wordsearch

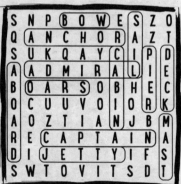

Page 84 – Spot the Difference   Page 85 – Wordwheel

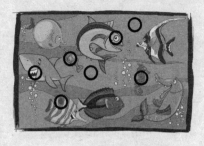

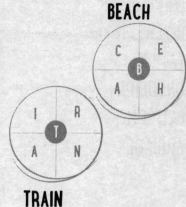

BEACH

C E
B
A H

I R
T
A N

TRAIN

Page 86 – Kriss Kross   Page 87 – Arrow Word

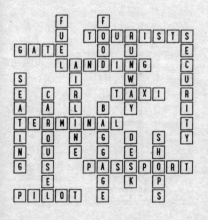

		S		E	
B	A	A		X	
	P	L	A	T	E
R	E	T	U	R	N
		S	A	D	
L	I	F	T		
	R		R	O	B
D	I	V	I	D	E
	S		A	D	D

Page 88 – Missing Vowels

TICKET
DRIVER
STATION
CONDUCTOR
PLATFORM
CARRIAGE

Page 89 – Quiz

1. c – The Big Apple
2. b – Paris
3. a – Cheetah
4. a – Black and white
5. c – More than 70 %
6. b – Leaning
7. b – Big Ben
8. c – Egypt

Page 90 – Pairs Match

Page 91 – Domino Match

Page 92 – Wordsearch

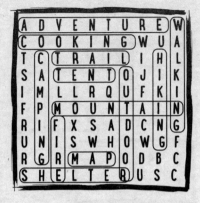

Page 93 – Maze

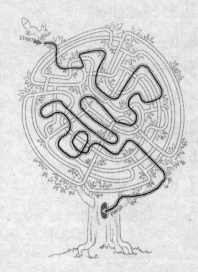

Page 94 – Wordwheel

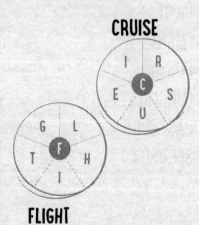

CRUISE

FLIGHT

Page 95 – Kriss Kross

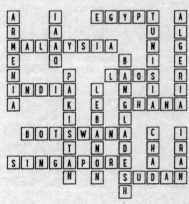

Page 96 – Quiz

1. a – California
2. b – Croissant
3. a – A torch
4. b – RMS Titanic
5. a – Hover
6. b – Drone
7. c – A saddle
8. c – Submarine

Page 97 – Sudoku

1	3	2	4
2	4	1	3
4	1	3	2
3	2	4	1

2	4	1	3
3	1	4	2
4	2	3	1
1	3	2	4

Page 98 – Domino Match

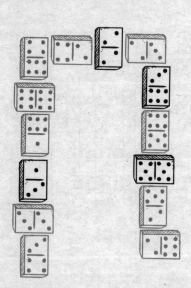

Page 99 – Missing Vowels

PILOT
FLIGHT
CUSTOMS
LUGGAGE
PASSPORT
SECURITY

Page 100 – Pairs Match

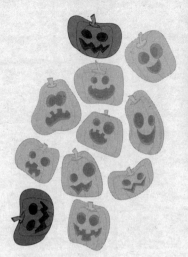

Page 101 – Wordsearch

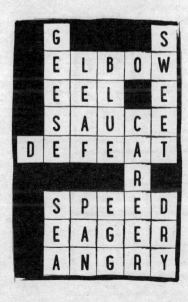

Page 102 – Arrow Word

G				S
E	L	B	O	W
E	E	L		E
S	A	U	C	E
D	E	F	E	A	T
			R	
S	P	E	E	D
E	A	G	E	R
A	N	G	R	Y

Page 103 – Quiz

1. b – Sahara
2. a – Peru
3. b – Canada
4. a – Great Wall of China
5. b – Tokyo
6. a – River Nile
7. c – Eucalyptus
8. c – Amazon

Page 104 – Spot the Difference   Page 105 – Domino Match

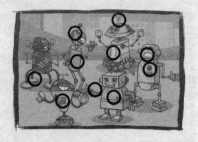

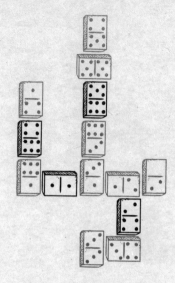

Page 106 – Kriss Kross   Page 107 – Sudoku

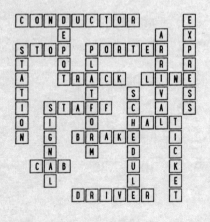

4	1	2	3
3	2	1	4
2	4	3	1
1	3	4	2

4	2	3	1
1	3	4	2
3	1	2	4
2	4	1	3

Page 108 – Maze

Page 109 – Wordwheel

LUGGAGE

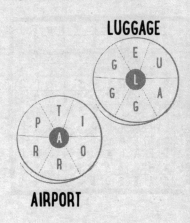

AIRPORT

Page 110 – Quiz

1. b – Glamping
2. c – Black
3. c – Skates
4. c – Motorway
5. a – Canter
6. c – Tricycle
7. a – Camel
8. c – Asia

Page 111 – Pairs Match

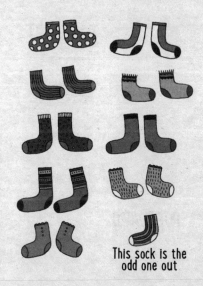

This sock is the odd one out

Page 112 – Wordsearch

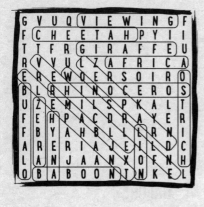

Page 113 – Missing Vowels

HOTEL

RELAX

TRAVEL

FAMILY

SUNSHINE

SIGHTSEE

Page 114 – Wordwheel

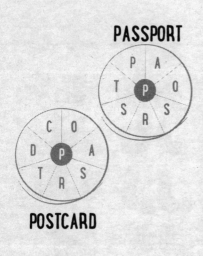

PASSPORT

POSTCARD

Page 115 – Arrow Word

					O
L	A	M	B		V
	R	A	I	S	E
	E	N	T	E	R
D	A	Y		R	
			L	I	E
A	C	T	I	O	N
	A		M	U	D
	P	R	E	S	S

Page 116 – Sudoku

2	3	5	6	4	1
4	1	6	5	2	3
5	4	2	3	1	6
3	6	1	4	5	2
1	5	3	2	6	4
6	2	4	1	3	5

Page 117 – Quiz

1. c – Red
2. b – Leek
3. b – The Tower of London
4. b – Pisa
5. b – Spain
6. c – New Delhi
7. b – Bread
8. c – Suriname

Page 118 – Domino Match

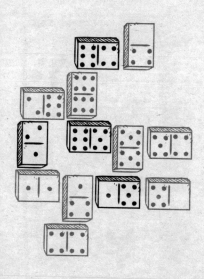

Page 119 – Kriss Kross

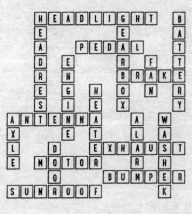

Page 120 - Arrow Word

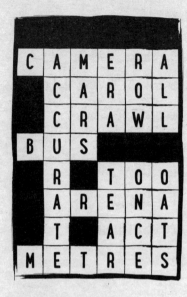

C	A	M	E	R	A		A
	C	A	R	O	L		L
	C	R	A	W	L		L
B	U	S					
	R			T	O	O	O
	A	R	E	N	A		A
	T			A	C	T	T
M	E	T	R	E	S		S

Page 121 - Missing Vowels

TRUCK
SERVICES
ROADWORKS
MOTORWAY
SEATBELT
COUNTRYSIDE

Page 122 - Maze

Page 123 - Pairs Match

146

Page 124 – Quiz

1. a – Portuguese
2. a – Kangaroo
3. b – Key lime pie
4. b – Red and white
5. a – A sandstone rock
6. c – Rink
7. c – Eiffel Tower (300 m)
8. a – Periscope

Page 125 – Wordwheel

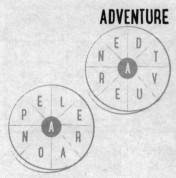

ADVENTURE

AEROPLANE

Page 126 – Wordsearch

Page 127 – Sudoku

5	4	3	1	2	6
1	6	2	5	4	3
6	3	1	4	5	2
4	2	5	6	3	1
2	5	6	3	1	4
3	1	4	2	6	5

Page 128 – Spot the Difference   Page 129 – Arrow Word

Page 130 – Kriss Kross

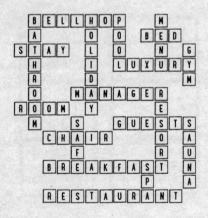

Page 131 – Missing Vowels

WAVES

TOWEL

SHELL

PARASOL

SUN CREAM

SANDCASTLE

Page 132 – Domino Match   Page 133 – Pairs Match

NOTES

NOTES

NOTES

NOTES

NOTES

NOTES

NOTES